Pieces of Another World
The Story of Moon Rocks

Pieces of Another World
World
The Story of Moon Rocks

By FRANKLYN M. BRANLEY

Illustrated by Herbert Danska

Thomas Y. Crowell Company

New York

9868

BY THE AUTHOR

The Christmas Sky
Experiments in Sky Watching
Man in Space to the Moon
The Mystery of Stonehenge
The Nine Planets
Pieces of Another World: The Story of
Moon Rocks

Photographs on pages 20, 22, 23, and 24 are from *Lunar Rocks Under the Microscope* by W. von Engelhardt and D. Stoffler, published by Optische Werke Carl Zeiss, 7082 Oberkochen, West Germany.

Photographs on pages i, 26, 27, 28, and 34 are from the National Aeronautics and Space Administration.

Designed by Joan Maestro

Manufactured in the United States of America

L.C. Card 71-158684

ISBN 0-690-62565-0
0-690-62566-9 (LB)

4 5 6 7 8 9 10

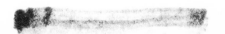

Contents

1 ◆ Collecting the Rocks 1

2 ◆ The Lunar Receiving Laboratory 12

3 ◆ Rocks, Dust, and Crystals 20

4 ◆ An Answer from the Moon Rocks 30

5 ◆ Some Questions Raised by Moon Rocks 33

6 ◆ The Moon's Origin and History 47

For Further Reading 55

Index 56

1

Collecting the Rocks

Earliest records tell us that men have always dreamed of escaping from the earth and traveling to other worlds. The dream vehicles they chose were baskets towed by fabulous birds, or blown by the wind, or carried by currents of hot air, or pulled by magnets. One poet said that if cups of dew were fastened to a person's waist, he would be lifted to the moon as the dew evaporated. Such dreams were fantasies, the stuff fairy tales are made of.

At 10:56 P.M. (E.D.T.) on July 20, 1969, these fantastic dreams became reality. On that day, Neil A. Armstrong, commander of Apollo 11, stepped onto the surface of the moon from Eagle, the lunar ship that had landed only moments before on Mare Tranquillitatis—the Sea of Tranquillity. Man had broken the bonds that for more than a million years had held him to the earth. He had set foot on another world.

Two lunar probes, Ranger and Surveyor, had landed on the moon before Apollo 11. When they did, people wondered if the ships would sink into the deep dust that some scientists believed covered the moon. But the ships had survived, and the LM (the lunar module that had carried Armstrong and Edwin A. Aldrin,

1

Jr., his fellow crew member) had sunk in only an inch or so. Nevertheless, Armstrong's first step was slow and careful. He was the first man to step onto another world, and no one knew what that world was like. Armstrong did not sink into the surface, however. Beneath a thin, dusty layer, the footing was firm and solid.

Once on the moon, Armstrong's first job was to pick up a sample of lunar rocks and soil, for one important purpose of the Apollo 11 mission was to bring back pieces of the moon. By studying them, scientists hoped to learn more about the history of the moon and the earth, the way they came into being, the changes that have occurred in them down through millenniums of time, and the changes that might occur in the future.

The astronauts were to spend two or three hours outside their ship. But if leaks developed in their space suits, or oxygen pressure dropped, or carbon dioxide built up too rapidly—if any of a thousand or more equipment functions failed to operate properly—their time outside the ship would have to be cut. The

scientists wanted to be sure that at least a few pieces of the moon would be brought back to earth, so Armstrong picked up samples of moon rocks as soon as he could.

The rocks picked up first were called the contingency sample. There were many uncertainties in the mission because the moon landing was a pioneering venture, and no one could possibly know what contingencies might arise to prevent the astronauts from getting more moon rocks.

Armstrong could not bend over because of his bulky space suit, and to pick up the first rocks he used a plastic bag attached to a hoop at the end of a collapsible rod, somewhat like a small fish net. He scooped up bits of moon dust and rocks into the bag. Then he removed the rod from the bag and awkwardly, because of the space suit, rolled up the bag and stuffed it into a pocket on the left leg of his space suit. This sample was

gathered from a small area only 5 feet away from the lunar module.

Nineteen minutes later Edwin Aldrin joined Neil Armstrong on the lunar surface. One of their assignments was to fill a box with lunar rocks. The two men could not move easily, nor could they bend over, so they used special tools to pick up the rocks. One of these tools was an aluminum scoop with a short handle. An extension handle snapped onto the short section, making it possible to pick up rocks and dust from a slightly bent position.

A second tool was a pair of tongs for picking up larger stones which could not fit inside the scoop. The tongs had a handle-plunger arrangement that made it possible for the astronaut to hold the tongs and operate them with one hand. The third tool was a hammer for breaking pieces of rock off large boulders. The hammer was designed to fit the same extension handle that was used for the scoop.

The astronauts carried cameras suspended in front of them,

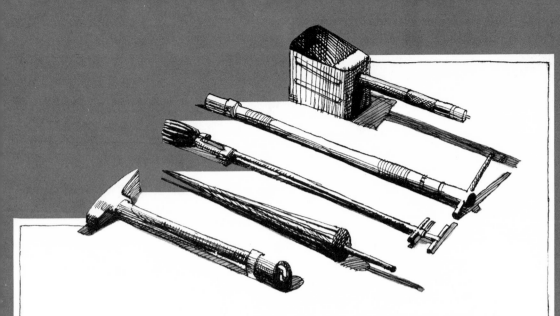

and also a stereo camera mounted near the end of a rod which was carried like a cane. This camera was designed to take three-dimensional close-up pictures of 3-inch-square areas of the lunar surface. When the rod was pushed down, a strobe flash went off and two pictures were taken. The camera was very close to the ground, so it could "see" surface details much better than the astronauts themselves, who could not bend over.

As Armstrong and Aldrin walked on the lunar surface collecting samples, they talked with one another by radio and with Mission Control at Houston, which was watching them by television. Here are some of their words:

ARMSTRONG: Now this one's right down front. And I want to know if you can see an angular rock in the foreground.

HOUSTON: Roger, we have a large angular rock in the foreground. And it looks like a much smaller rock a couple of inches to the left.

ARMSTRONG: And beyond it about 10 feet is an even larger

rock that's rounded. That rock is about—the closest one to you is about—that one sticking out of the sand—about one foot. It's about a foot and a half long and it's about 6 inches thick. But it's standing on edge.

HOUSTON: Roger, and we see the shadow of the LM.

ARMSTRONG: Just beyond the shadow of the LM is a pair of elongated craters, so they appear together as 40 feet long and 20 feet across, and they're probably 6 feet deep. We'll probably get more work in there later.

Aldrin and Armstrong had many chores to do, including erecting experimental apparatus to measure moon temperature and moon tremors and determine the composition of the solar wind. They were also to display the American flag, photograph the LM and themselves, and collect about 25 pounds (earth weight) of rocks, which they were to place in an air-tight container to be brought back to earth. Samples were scooped up randomly out to about 35 feet from the base of the LM. The astronauts wanted to get samples from beyond the LM because those close to it might have been affected by the exhaust of the rocket engines as the LM came in for a landing.

The second group of rocks was called the bulk sample. It was placed in one of two similar metal boxes, which were like small suitcases with triple air-tight seals. A ring of indium, a soft metal, lined the edge of each box. When the box was filled, the lid was closed, and the sharp edge of the lid cut into the indium, making a tight, leak-proof seal. Heavy straps were buckled securely to hold the seal. The box was then wrapped in a plastic bag.

6

Later, Armstrong collected rocks to fill the second container. This was called the documented sample, because these rocks were specially selected rather than scooped up at random.

Armstrong occasionally angled the scoop so that it dug down about 3 inches below the surface. The "soil" remained about the same to that depth; there was no hard crust to break through. There were rocks of all sizes, and a good many were about 2 feet across, too large to fit into the cases.

While Armstrong was collecting the rocks, Aldrin was pounding hollow tubes into the moon so he could collect samples from underneath the surface layer. He had no trouble getting the tube down 3 inches, but then he could go deeper only by pounding as hard as he could.

At Mission Control the men thought a moon rock had jammed the tube. It was important to get samples from as deep as possible, because the blast from the LM engines might have affected the rocks at or near the surface. Aldrin pounded the tube in about 9 inches, but it would not stay erect. It would fall over unless it was supported. Scientists could not understand why the tube had to be pounded so hard when the lunar "soil" seemed so loose. They still don't know why. The "soil" was not firm enough to hold the tube erect, probably because the particles slid over one another, acting more or less like round grains of dry sand.

Aldrin said, "The tube didn't seem to want to stand upright. I'd keep drawing it in and it would dig some sort of a hole, but it wouldn't penetrate in a way that it would support itself." Later

8

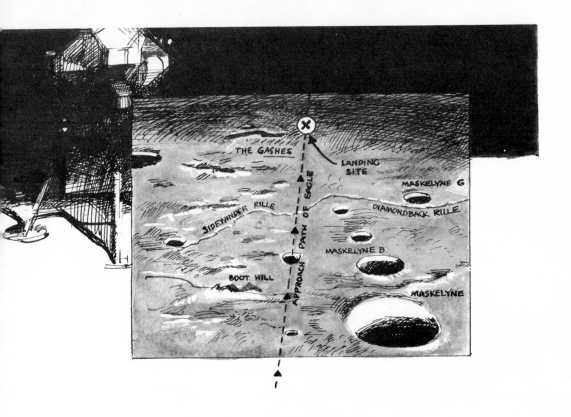

he said that "the material in the tube was quite well packed, a good bit darker, and the way it adhered to the core tube gave me the distinct impression of being moist."

The moistness that Aldrin referred to was not water, because as far as we can determine at this time, there is no free water on the moon. Some people believe that when we explore the moon more extensively we'll find ice in deep lunar crevices into which sunlight never enters. This may be so, but so far no water has been identified. The appearance of wetness was probably due to the fineness of the lunar "soil."

Armstrong mentioned the peculiar appearance of the surface material in this description transmitted to Mission Control at Houston: "We are landed in a relatively clear crater field . . . of

circular secondary craters, most of which have rims. . . . There are a few of the smaller craters around, which do not have a discernible rim. The ground mass throughout the area is a very fine sand to a silt. I'd say the thing that would be most like it on earth is powdered graphite.'' Graphite in the solid form is the ''lead'' in a pencil. We see it in powdered form when the graphite is used as a lubricant. It is somewhat shiny and looks greasy.

After they were filled, the sample containers were stowed with care aboard the LM, treated as though they held the most precious jewels imaginable. And in a sense they did. For the first time in man's history he had set foot on another world and gathered some pieces of that world. Now the task remained to get these pieces of the moon back to the earth safely. Then scientists would be able to analyze them to determine their structure and perhaps trace their history.

At 1:55 P.M. (E.D.T.) on Monday, July 21, the upper part of the LM separated from its launching platform (the lower part of the module). It lifted off from Tranquillity Base and carried Armstrong and Aldrin to a rendezvous with Colonel Michael Collins, who had been orbiting the moon while Armstrong and Aldrin were on the lunar surface. The men and the moon rocks were transferred from the LM to the command module. Then the LM was jettisoned and the rocket engines aboard the service module were fired. Apollo 11 was on its journey back to earth with its precious cargo of pieces of another world.

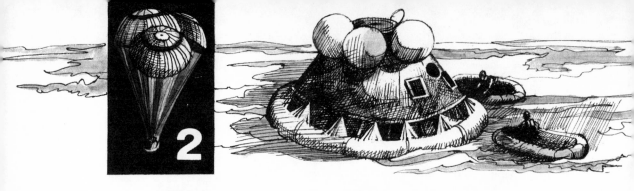

The Lunar Receiving Laboratory

Immediately after splashdown in the Pacific Ocean, the sample cases were flown by jet to Ellington Air Force Base near Houston, Texas, and then rushed to the Lunar Receiving Laboratory (LRL).

The LRL is a large building located at one of the corners of a large complex of buildings called the Manned Spacecraft Center just outside Houston. The laboratory was designed as a place where the astronauts would be quarantined—kept isolated for 21 days to be sure they had not brought disease-causing lunar organisms back to the earth—and where the lunar rocks and soil would be exposed to earth's environment and the first studies made of the composition and structure of the rocks. Powerful vacuum pumps were installed in the building, as were microscopes, spectrometers, remote handling equipment, chemistry laboratories, and every conceivable type of equipment that might be needed by the 26 scientists who would make preliminary examinations of the rocks.

Most of the scientists were geologists. There were spectroscopists, who are specialists in identifying rocks and the minerals they are made of, and there were experts on many kinds of rocks: volcanic rocks; metamorphic rocks—that is, rocks which have

12

been changed by temperature, stress, or pressure; and impact rocks—rocks formed by collisions.

Astronomers who had spent their lives studying the moon were there, and so were chemists and biologists and physicists; some of the men knew a great deal about magnetism in rocks, and others were students of meteorites and tektites, the small glassy bodies that some experts think may be of meteoritic origin.

These 26 scientists studied the rocks before they were released to other investigators around the world, but they did not touch them. Handling was done only in gloved compartments, in either a vacuum or an atmosphere of dry nitrogen. The scientists examined the rocks, photographed them, weighed them, and chipped them for chemical and physical analyses and biological testing. The rocks were exposed to gases, and the scientists determined the minerals in them and whether or not they contained any organic carbon, an essential for life.

Time was important because the scientists wanted to study the rocks as soon as possible after they were removed from the lunar environment. The minute the rocks were taken from the moon, they were subjected to conditions different from those that had prevailed during the previous millions of years: they were jostled about, they were in a stronger gravitational field, and they were exposed to a much stronger magnetic field.

Scientists had planned delicate investigations of the magnetism of the rocks, if any, to give them clues about the presence of a magnetic pole on the moon and to reveal the kinds of gases, if any, given off by the rocks. The longer their work was delayed, the greater was the possibility of losing valuable traces of information or of having it contaminated by earthly conditions.

This was the first time that material from another world had been brought back to earth. No one knew for sure what to expect. Would the moon rocks be dangerous? It was possible that deadly chemicals or bacteria might be encased in the lunar rocks or embedded in the lunar "soil."

Some people recalled reading about the terrible epidemic that had spread across the Fiji Islands in 1875, and they feared that the same thing might happen again, but this time on a global scale. Cakobau, who was king of the islands at that time, made a trip to nearby Australia and while there became sick with measles. Still sick, the king returned to the Fiji Islands, and the disease spread rapidly to thousands of other people. Ordinarily, measles is not deadly, but the Fiji Islanders had no resistance to the disease—that is, no way of fighting measles because they had never been exposed to it. Before the epidemic ended, 40,000 people had died. People on earth would be just as vulnerable to a disease brought by new and deadly bacteria contained in moon rocks.

No one really expected the moon rocks to cause such a calamity, but they had to take every precaution nevertheless. The Lunar Receiving Laboratory was designed to provide every precaution. It was also designed to keep the moon rocks in an environment as similar as possible to that on the moon until they could be changed from lunar conditions to those on earth with complete safety.

When the lunar-sample boxes were received at the lab, everyone wanted to open them immediately, so great was their excitement. But the outer surfaces had to be sterilized first to remove any contamination acquired on the earth, so the boxes were moved through chambers from which air was removed. As they moved, the pressure was gradually lowered, until it approached the vacuum that exists on the moon. Ultraviolet light was shone on the boxes to kill any bacteria that might be on the exterior, and the surfaces were washed with acid sprays to clean them thoroughly. Then nitrogen gas was introduced to dry the cases.

After the pressure was dropped to as near zero as possible and the boxes had been sterilized, a technician working outside the chamber placed his hands inside glove ports, which enabled him to work on the cases without disturbing the high vacuum that surrounded them. Study of the moon rocks was about to begin. Somewhat awkwardly, the technician picked up a hollow needle fastened to the end of a hose and punctured seals in the side of the box. Any gases that had been collected on the moon, or that might have come out of the rocks during the journey, would go through the needle to the hose and then to a mass spectrometer, an instrument that is used to identify gases by the mass of the atoms they are made of.

The technician moved slowly and deliberately. No errors must be made. To make sure that whatever gases were in the cases had been collected, the scientists waited impatiently for more than an hour before doing anything else. No gases were identified, which meant that no earth gases had leaked into the cases, that the moon rocks did not release gases, and that no gases had been scooped up by the astronauts as they collected the rock and soil samples.

Then it was time to open the cases and for the scientists to get their first look at these pieces of another world. Every one of these 26 men wanted to be looking when the seal of the case was broken, but this was impossible, so they watched on closed-circuit television. The scientists who were alongside the technician explained what was happening as the boxes were opened.

The technician picked up the unlatching tool and got it into position. His hands were still inside the gloves that ballooned into the vacuum chamber.

At 3:49 P.M. on July 25, 1969, the seal was broken.

The technician lifted the lid and put it aside. All the men saw was padding, the packing material that had kept the rocks from bouncing. When the padding was removed they saw a plastic bag containing aluminum foil. This was the solar wind experiment that the astronauts had erected to pick up particles ejected from the sun.

The plastic bag was placed on top of the lid. The technician slowly, deliberately, moved the box so he could reach into it. Then, carefully, he removed a core tube, one of the hollow tubes that Aldrin had hammered into the surface of the moon.

Still, no one had seen a moon rock. They were inside another plastic bag, the one in which Armstrong had placed them. The technician reached into a tool box inside the chamber and picked up a razor to cut open the bag.

Later, a scientist commented on that moment: "When we opened that first box of moon rocks, the hushed, expectant atmosphere in the Lunar Receiving Laboratory was, I imagine, like that in a medieval monastery as the monks awaited the arrival of a fragment of the true cross."

The technician slit the bag open. At first, all the men could see was black dust and grime and, here and there, a solid chunk of dark-gray rock. In texture and color the moon rocks looked like uneven charcoal briquets, and the dust looked like briquets that had been ground to powder.

This first look revealed nothing that could be identified. Later on, when seen under a microscope and investigated more carefully, the rocks offered many mysteries.

Geologists were amazed to find that the dust and grime contained large numbers of tiny beads of glass. Some of the rocks were filled with small holes and cavities that apparently had been produced by the expansion and cooling of molten rock. They looked like basalt, a volcanic rock found in the earth. There were tiny indentations in the rocks, perhaps caused by meteoritic bombardments. And here and there the scientists saw small, shiny, black crystals. There were also rocks which looked as though they were made of many rocks cemented together.

Biologists were eager to expose the rocks to every kind of test to find if they contained any clues to the presence of life on the moon—either today or at any time during its history of millions of years.

Some geologists wanted to split rocks open to see their internal structure. Others wanted to heat samples and change them to gases to find out what elements they were made of. Still others hoped to slice some of the rocks into thin wafers so that light could be passed through them, revealing their crystal structure. Other scientists wanted to weigh the rocks, scratch them, pound them, measure their magnetism, expose them to every conceivable investigation. And they did.

After the 26 scientists at the LRL had begun their work and made their first report, more than a hundred scientists from around the world arrived in Houston. Each was given a few grains of lunar "soil" or tiny bits of moon rock to take back to his own laboratory. Six months later they returned their samples to Houston, where they assembled in a grand meeting to report on the work they had done and what they had learned about the moon rocks.

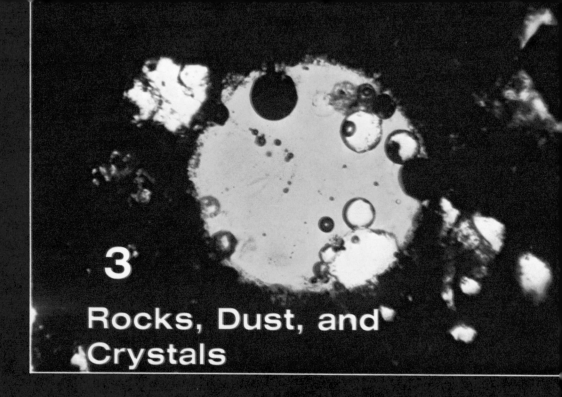

3

Rocks, Dust, and Crystals

LUNAR ROCKS

Scientists divided the lunar rocks that were to be studied into four groups. The first group was made up of igneous rocks—that is, rocks formed by the action of heat. They have rather small crystals and little depressions or cavities, and are very similar to the basalt found on earth, dark in color and fine-grained. In the second group were igneous rocks with larger cavities, which are often lined with glassy material. They are similar to dolerite and are dark and coarse-grained. Microbreccias, masses of small rocks cemented or melted together, made up the third group. The fourth group consisted of very small grains of material, less than a centimeter in diameter, called fines. This group included the tiny glass spheres and crystals found in the lunar soil.

The rocks have two characteristics that are peculiar to moon rocks: they contain small pits that are lined with glass, and there are spatters of glassy material on some of them that do not appear to be related to the pits. The pits are very small, averaging only a millimeter across (there are 25 millimeters in one inch). These glass surfaces are shiny and usually quite uneven in shape. Geologists think these pits and spatters of glass may have been made by direct impacts of particles traveling at high speeds, or they might be the result of indirect but nearby impacts.

Rocks from Apollo 11 and 12 fit into these four groups. However, there are differences between the two cargoes. Apollo 11 rocks are about half igneous, with small and large crystals, and half microbreccia, while the Apollo 12 samples are mostly crystalline. Scientists believe this is because the Apollo 12 rocks were collected from a region that is either right on a crater rim or very close to the rim. It is believed that at such locations the lunar crust is rather thin, and so the rocks may be from the bedrock of the moon. The Apollo 11 rocks are from a region where the bedrock is covered over, and therefore these samples are of rocks that probably were broken up into small pieces and then welded together. (The Apollo 14 rocks are from the Fra Mauro region, a rough, irregular area strewn with loose boulders.)

As far as their composition is concerned, the rocks in both samples appear to be essentially the same. The main differences are in the percentage of ilmenite ($FeTiO_3$), a mineral rich in titanium. The Apollo 12 rocks contain less ilmenite than those of Apollo 11, and a greater abundance of olivine (Mg_2SiO_4).

The principal minerals found in the lunar rocks are pyroxene, plagioclase, ilmenite, and olivine. Pyroxene contains silicon and

oxygen, and calcium, iron, or magnesium. In the coarse moon rocks one can see it as bright, brownish grains about a sixteenth of an inch across.

Plagioclase feldspar is made mostly of aluminum, silicon, oxygen, calcium, and sodium. Some of the minerals indicate that they have been exposed to extreme shock, perhaps caused by the impact of meteorites. Similar minerals have been found on the earth near meteorite craters and in regions that have been affected by nuclear explosions.

A real surprise to geologists was the abundance of ilmenite in the lunar rocks. Ilmenite is found on the earth, but it rarely exceeds 5 percent of the rocks in which it is found. As much as 20 percent of moon rocks is ilmenite. The mineral is easily detected in moon rocks because it appears as shiny black grains

Opposite page: A sampling of lunar rocks, here enlarged from their microscopic size.

or crystals. If ilmenite is heated to a high temperature and then cooled rapidly, small amounts of zirconium can be detected. Some of the moon rocks were found to contain zirconium, which indicates that there was high heat and fast cooling on some regions of the moon.

Olivine was found to be a major part of the Apollo 12 rocks. It appears as colorless grains when the rocks are sliced thin and observed under a microscope. Olivine is also found on the earth,

Tiny glass sphere, 1 mm across (25.4 mm = 1 inch).

Tiny glass sphere in breccia.

although the chemical composition of lunar olivine is somewhat different from that of the terrestrial variety, which contains larger amounts of calcium and chromium.

Many other minerals are found in lunar rocks, though in lesser amounts. There are some differences between the lunar-rock minerals and those in earth rocks—the percentage of ilmenite, the larger amount of calcium in olivine, the presence of zirconium—but there are many similarities in the minerals, especially in the composition of major chemicals that make up the minerals.

Lunar igneous rocks, or basalts, both fine-grained and coarse, appear to be volcanic in nature. Apparently they were entirely molten at one time. The small gas cavities—some round and smooth, others quite uneven and lined with crystals—indicate that this was the case. Also, the rocks appear to be volcanic for the most part. They must have cooled very near the surface of the moon, or perhaps at the surface. When molten rock cools rapidly, the crystals are small. Many of the crystals in the lunar basalts are small, not unlike many basaltic lavas found on the earth.

The lunar basalts that contain larger crystals took a long time to cool. They may have been in the bottom part of a lava flow or in the lava that pushed up from underneath but never broke through the surface.

The small and large cavities or pits in the basalts indicate that gases were released from the melted rock during an eruption through the surface or during a push very near the surface. It is quite impossible, from the evidence in the basalts themselves, to determine what the escaped gases were.

A study of the structure of rocks and of their present magnetic properties (or lack of them) provides clues to the magnetic history of the rocks. Earth rocks show a magnetic history that is related to the over-all magnetic field of the earth that results from the semimolten layer of the planet.

There are indications of magnetic fields (crystal formations) that may have existed in the moon long ago, but so far it cannot be proved whether or not the moon ever had a molten interior. The magnetism that produced the formations could have resulted from meteorite impacts. An iron bar, for example, can be magnetized by pounding it and demagnetized by pounding.

In the Apollo 14 mission rocks were collected in a more carefully recorded fashion and this will be the procedure in the future. Scientists will know the position of the rock in relation to the lunar poles. This will give them additional data to help them understand the crystal structure and arrangement they observe.

25

If they knew the age of the moon, astronomers would be in a better position to develop theories of how the moon came into existence and what its history is. Therefore, there was much interest in dating the lunar rocks. This was done by measuring the breakdown of radioactive elements, such as lead to thorium, rubidium to strontium, and potassium to argon. Seven of the rocks tested were found to be between 2.3 and 3.7 billion years old—very old when compared to most earth rocks, the oldest of which, samples found in Southern Rhodesia, are about 2.7 billion years old.

More interesting was the fact that the lunar rocks were not all the same age. The oldest turned out to be a small piece—less than half an inch across, found at Tranquillity Base, but which may have come from beyond the area—that is 4.4 billion years old. Most of the rocks from Tranquillity (Apollo 11) are about 3.7 billion years old. The Apollo 12 rocks are younger—about 2.3 to 3.3 billion years old. This range in age may mean that the moon was volcanic for a long, long time during its early history.

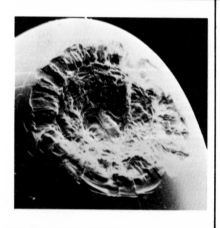 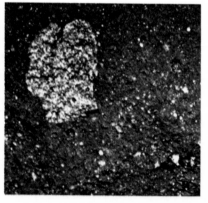

Small craters are found in many samples of lunar material. Small shiny patches were probably formed by intense heating.

Basalt (volcanic) and breccia (loose materials cemented together) are common on the moon.

LUNAR "SOIL"

The flat regions of the moon (if we can generalize from Apollo 11) appear to be covered with relatively loose material to a depth of 12 feet or so, on the average. The material has been called lunar soil, but it bears no similarity to earth soil. Therefore, geologists would rather refer to it as the lunar regolith—*lith* meaning rock and *rego* meaning blanket. It is made of the lunar fines mentioned earlier.

The Apollo 11 astronauts could discern four different zones in the regolith: (1) a thin, light-gray layer of dust about an eighth of an inch thick; (2) a thin, caked layer about a quarter of an inch deep that cracked 5 or 6 inches away when stepped on; (3) a 5- to 6-inch layer of sandy, silty material that tended to "stick" together; (4) a layer similar to the third but which held together more firmly and was harder to penetrate.

Here and there on the moon the astronauts found no regolith at all; at those places the underlying basaltic rock had broken through to the surface.

The regolith is made of glass particles, fragments of basalts, and meteoritic material that has rained down on the moon for thousands and thousands of years.

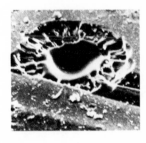

Tiny craters (some pinhead-size), probably formed by impact, occur frequently.

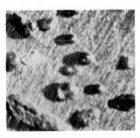

The lunar soil contains glass spheres of various colors, many only $1/25$" in diameter.

Small lunar rock, about $1\frac{1}{2}$" long. Appearance is much like terrestrial rocks.

The glass resulted from the impact force of meteorites. When a meteorite crashed on the moon, the regolith was melted and blobs of melted rock were thrown in all directions. The blobs sometimes solidified in flight and became perfectly formed spheres of different colors—red, amber, blue, green. The spheres are very small—a microscope is required to see their roundness. When the blobs of melted rock spattered onto the surface before cooling completely, they hardened into glassy formations in a multitude of different shapes and sizes, but all extremely small.

About half of the Apollo 11 samples were classified as microbreccias. *Micro* refers to the smallness of the fragments of which the substances are made, while *breccia* indicates that the grains of the rock are irregular rather than smooth and rounded.

The microbreccias appear to be made of regolith particles that have been welded together. It is believed that the heat that caused them to consolidate may have come either from bombardments by meteorites or from shock waves that generated tremendous heat and caused instant melting followed by rapid cooling.

The basaltic material of the Sea of Tranquillity appears to have originated in the bedrock of the area. The seas of the moon sometimes appear to be craters originally produced by the impact of meteorites. Then, still quite early in the history of the moon, vast lava flows filled these craters with basalt. Later, during millenniums of time, the solid basalt was broken down, crumbled, and reduced to fine particles. Finally, still later, meteorites cemented the particles into the breccias found by our astronauts.

Every day tons of meteoritic material fall on the earth. However, the meteorites break up, are buried, or are quickly weathered away. Similarly, tons of meteoritic material fall on the moon. Since there is no weathering, one might expect to find considerable debris there. However, meteorites falling on the moon are not slowed by an atmosphere, and their high velocity creates such tremendous heat on impact that they melt, and they also melt the region where they strike.

Geologists believe they have found remnants of meteorites in lunar "soil," and they are certain in a few cases. But most of the remnants cannot readily be separated from rocks and fines that originated in the moon itself. The amount of definitely identifiable meteoritic material found in the moon is a very small percentage of the total samples studied—much less than 1 percent.

As investigation of the 3 ounces of "soil" returned from the Sea of Fertility by Luna 16 and the more than 150 pounds of rock and "soil" returned by Apollo 11, 12, and 14 continues, and as samples from other regions of the moon are brought back to earth, we shall add to our growing knowledge of the nature of the moon rocks. Perhaps we'll find that many of the conclusions and hypotheses made so far will have to be modified. But there are some things we know for sure from our study of moon rocks, and one of the things we know is that life does not exist on the moon.

4

An Answer from the Moon Rocks

Since the Italian astronomer Giovanni Schiaparelli announced in the 1870's that he had seen "canals" on Mars, people have been fascinated by the possibility that life might exist there. And they have also conjectured about life on the moon.

The 26 scientists at the LRL, and the 140 teams who were loaned samples of moon rock, were eager to know if there was any sign of life on the moon today, or any clue that would indicate if life had ever existed there.

Biologists pulverized lunar rocks and dust and then mixed small amounts with the food fed to birds, fish, insects, and mice. Also, small amounts were injected into the muscles of test animals.

The mice used were germ-free. They had been born and raised in completely sterile surroundings, and so had no immunity to diseases. If there had been any disease-causing substance in the moon rocks, some of the 200 mice would have become sick. But none of them did. Neither did any of the other test animals.

As a control, earth rocks similar to the moon rocks were pulverized and injected into other test animals. In many cases these animals became sluggish and lazy, perhaps because the earth rocks were more soluble than moon rocks, and so were more readily taken in by the animals.

Since no test animals contracted any disease, and none of the astronauts showed any ill effects from the exposure to lunar dust that would have gotten into the landing vehicles, it is generally believed that the moon contains no living organisms. We now know there need be no fear of catching a lethal disease from moon rocks. Scientists working with them now do not have to wear masks, and the rocks do not have to be kept in a vacuum nor do they have to be sterilized.

Many scientists were surprised (and disappointed, too) by the absence of native organic materials on the moon. They didn't necessarily believe that life had originated on the moon, but they knew that the earth has a "tail" of gases and charged particles that extends thousands of miles into space. Occasionally the

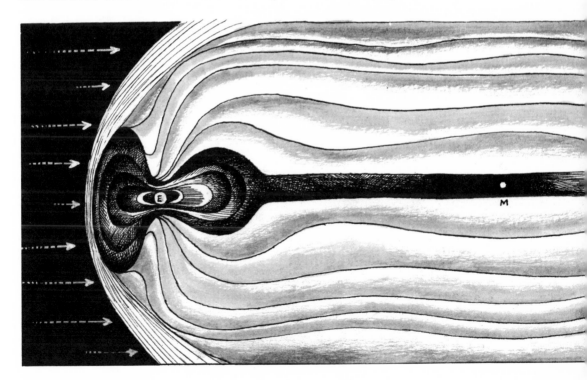

moon passes through this cloud of gases. These scientists reasoned that certain forms of life, such as bacteria, spores, and viruses, might have been ejected into space from the earth and that the organisms could have been caught up in earth's "tail" of gases and transported to the moon. Maybe they were, but if so, we have not been able to identify such organisms as yet.

But not all of the scientists went along with this theory. Before the pulverized moon rocks were fed to test animals and before they were exposed to microscopic study for the presence of organic material, one of the scientists at the LRL said, "The chance of bringing anything harmful back from the moon is probably one in a hundred billion. The chance of finding any living organism is about as small. None of the organisms we know could flourish on the moon, though some might be able to barely survive there. They couldn't start growth there, and they couldn't evolve."

It looks as though he was right.

People had been divided in their thinking about life on the moon. Some were convinced there was none; others were quite certain some kind of life would be found there. And many still feel we should not conclude from the small samples studied so far that there is no life there. We have samples from only three locations, not including the grains scooped up by the Russian probe. Probably instead of saying there is no life on the moon, we should say that *as far as we know* there is no life on this neighbor world of ours.

But lunar exploration raised many other questions; one of them concerns the small glass-lined depressions that were photographed by the astronauts.

5

Some Questions Raised by Moon Rocks

TINY GLAZED CRATERS

Besides the moon rocks, the astronauts brought back exciting photographs of the moon. Some of these, you recall, were taken with a camera which was mounted at the bottom of a canelike rod and took stereo pictures of an area only 3 inches square. When scientists studied these stereo pictures, they saw details never seen before, not even by the astronauts.

Within the 3-by-3-inch area scientists were surprised to find small glazed patches. The largest of these shiny glasslike patches was only half an inch wide. The region of the moon where Apollo 11 landed appears to be covered by tiny craters, maybe 2 or 3 inches across. Inside these craters are clumps of lunar "soil" which are usually toward the center of the crater and rise like columns from its floor. These clumps and columns appear to be material that was brushed into the craters some time after the craters were formed.

The tops of the columns are glazed, but not the sides. Also, the rims of the tiny craters often contain glazed patches, but the inner walls do not. Only the tops of formations are shiny.

Now that they've seen these glazed patches, scientists are challenged to explain them. How were they formed? What could have happened to produce them? Some scientists have theories that attempt to offer answers.

Obviously, there must have been intense heating to produce the glassy surfaces. The tremendous heat of the rocket engine exhaust might have caused the melting as the LM descended to the lunar surface, and so some of the scientists guessed that particles might have been melted and then blown away from the area directly below the ship.

However, while this idea sounds reasonable, observations made by the astronauts do not support it. The glazing was observed about 50 feet from the ship. This was far from the area disturbed by the LM, which was mainly the surface within the legs on which the LM rested. No melting was seen in this area.

Small, shiny pillars and shiny sections of tiny crater walls indicate flash heating of the moon to high temperatures.

Moreover, even if there had been melting and all the particles had been blown away by the rocket exhaust, one would expect the particles to be scattered along the surface. But the photographs show that they are not. In all cases, the shiny spots occur inside the small craters or in patches along the rim, and usually on the columns toward the centers of the craters.

Because of this, most of the people who have studied these photographs feel that the glazing was not caused by the heat of the LM landing engine.

Careful study of the photographs indicates that whatever caused the glazing, in many cases it came from the same direction. The glazed patches in a single group might all be on the right, for example, or the left. The side on which the glazing occurs might vary from one group to another, but within a particular group it would all be on one side.

Some scientists have suggested that the shiny patches may be drops of melted rock that were thrown into the area by an impact elsewhere on the moon. They say that a meteorite might have crashed into the moon's surface, causing enough heat to melt rocky surfaces and enough force to throw the particles several hundred feet. If this had happened one would expect the particles to be spread around on the surface, much as they would have been had the rocket engine produced them, but they were not. Also, the glazing is often just on the top of delicate columns of lunar soil that would crumble at the slightest touch or vibration. It's impossible to conceive how such fragile formations could have been produced, and continued to exist, had there been any appreciable splash effect such as would be made by a crashing meteorite.

It does not seem reasonable that all parts of the craters could have been glazed at one time and then, as the material was worn away, only the glazing on the clumps was left behind. If this had happened, the process of erosion would have filled in the craters rather than cleared them out. Glazing produced by the same forces that made the tiny craters doesn't seem reasonable either. An impact that could have produced the craters would not have left behind the delicate columns; they crumble too easily. The location of the glazing makes it appear more as though the tops, tips, and edges of the formations had been heated and that melting caused the material to flow together. If so, the heating would have to have come from some source other than impact.

One theory holds that the heating was produced by a tremendous meteorite that crashed into the moon. Certainly, high temperatures would have been produced by such an event—but the sides of small craters would have been sheltered from the heat

rather than exposed to it. If the heat had come from the lunar surface where the meteorite struck, it would have radiated in straight lines. Then the flat surfaces of the moon might have been glazed, but the heat would not have penetrated into crater holes.

Another theory suggests that a tremendous meteorite crashed into the earth some 50,000 to 60,000 years ago. The heat generated by such an impact would have been enough to cause earth-surface materials to melt, and sufficient heat might have been reflected to the moon to cause melting there in limited regions. In order to produce sufficient heat to do this, the meteorite would have had to be 2 or 3 miles in diameter.

Wind and water erosion on the earth smooths jagged crater walls and fills in deep craters with debris. But if a really gigantic meteorite had crashed into the earth 50,000 or even 100,000 years ago, erosion would not yet have destroyed all signs of it, and we would still be able to see variations in the contour of the land. Geologists have observed the entire earth from airplanes and with satellites, but careful study of their photographs reveals no trace of any such mammoth crater. So this theory does not seem to explain this moon mystery.

The heat source for the entire solar system is the sun. We know that the temperature of the sun has varied. Perhaps for a minute or two the heat of the sun had become abnormally intense. If so, where the heat from the sun had struck a surface of the moon at a 90-degree angle it would have been most intense and could have caused melting of the lunar soil. Where the angle was less than 90 degrees, the heat would have bounced from the surface. This would account for the fact that the glazed areas occur in a patchy fashion rather than evenly. Also, if the sun's energy had increased greatly for only a minute or so there would not have been enough time for the heat to penetrate deep into the lunar soil—only the outer material would have melted, just as we find to be the case with the patches. The glazed surface is very thin.

Whether the sun produced the heat or something else did, the event must have happened only 50,000 to 100,000 years ago. The moon is bombarded constantly by the small bits of matter that abound in lunar space, and they would have broken down the fragile pillars and mounds if the pillars and mounds were more than 100,000 years old. Therefore, the heating must have occurred very recently—that is, "recently" in relation to the age of the moon.

This raises the question of whether the sun could have caused such intense heating for so short a period of time, or if there is some other explanation. The sun is an active, dynamic star.

Changes occur on it constantly; sunspots come and go, great streamers of glowing hydrogen gas erupt from its surface, small localized areas suddenly increase in brightness. But the sun is so gigantic, and the heat it generates is so tremendous, that these changes produce no significant variation in the amount of energy produced. Scientists believe that for millions of years the sun has been as bright as it is today, but no brighter.

Chances are that there is flare activity on the sun at this moment, but we would not be aware of it. Solar telescopes are needed to observe these flares. Many millions of years ago there may have been more violent activity, but we cannot be sure unless, as some scientists have suggested, the shiny patches are evidence that there were super-flares which might have been extensive enough to increase by 100 times the energy radiated by the sun.

The solar-flare theory seems reasonable to many people who have studied the sun and its evolution, but there is another possible explanation for the sudden increase in heat. Some scientists think it is possible that the sun may have exploded. Astronomers know of many stars that have exploded and then disappeared, and there are other stars that have exploded, quieted down, and then exploded again.

Such stars are called novas, or super-novas. *Nova* is the Latin word for new, and it is used because in ancient times people thought such stars were new ones. In many cases these stars had not been observed previously, so men quite naturally considered them to be newly created.

Even though our sun is not a nova—that is, it is not the type of star that explodes—astronomers readily admit that they do not know all there is to know about the stars, including the sun. Perhaps there have been occasions during the lifetime of the sun when it has suddenly burst forth in super-brilliance for fleeting moments. If this has happened the heat would surely have been great enough to produce the glassy patches on the moon.

There is still another theory that tries to account for the sudden heating of the moon which is indicated by these glazed patches. This theory concerns collisions between the sun and an asteroid or comet. There are probably millions of comets in the solar system. Comets are made mostly of gases that are quite concentrated in the nucleus, or core, of the comet, where vast amounts of cosmic dust and particles are also clustered. Comets move in orbits that occasionally take them close to the sun, and it is possible that the sun's gravitational attraction would be great enough to pull in a nearby comet.

It is also reasonable to suppose that an asteroid might have

been pulled into the sun. Asteroids are masses of rock and metal that range in size from as small as a marble to 500 miles across. In the past, there probably were hundreds of thousands of them, moving generally in an orbit between Mars and Jupiter. Occasionally an asteroid is deflected from its orbit and may be pulled in close to the sun. On rare occasions, asteroids may actually have disappeared into the sun.

The sun is a medium-hot star, having a surface temperature that is about 6,000 degrees centigrade. But the atmosphere of the sun (its outer envelope of gases) is much hotter—a million degrees and more. At such high temperatures, any matter that entered the sun's atmosphere would be converted into energy. The total amount would be staggering, but the effect would last only a few moments.

Suppose there had been such a gigantic outburst of energy— how would the earth have fared? Scientists believe that the earth has had its protective blanket of atmosphere for millions of years. And, possibly, at the time the solar bursts may have happened, the atmosphere acted as a buffer, insulating the earth's surface from the fury of the blast so that we would not find any signs of the event here on the earth. We expect that Venus would not have been affected either, and for the same reason—a dense atmosphere shields the planet.

Mercury and Mars, however, would have been affected severely. The atmosphere of Mars was probably rather thin throughout most of the planet's history, and a solar flare-up would have developed pressure enough to blow it away. Although the red planet has an atmosphere now, scientists think the gases originated in the planet itself rather than having been captured from outer space by the planet's gravitational attraction. So this atmosphere would have formed after the flare-up. Someday, when we can collect and analyze samples of Martian gases, we may be able to determine their origin. If the gases are traced to the Martian interior, as we expect, the theory of a solar burst that would have blown away the gases associated with the planet's formation will be strengthened.

Mercury, being the planet nearest the sun—only 36 million miles from it, would have been most affected by the blast. It's possible that half of Mercury—the face that was turned toward the sun at that moment—is entirely glazed. Scientists hope to send vehicles to Mercury to photograph the planet, and eventually they hope to be able to land vehicles, collect samples, and either return them to earth or transmit to earth analyses performed by automated instruments aboard the landing vehicle.

It would be exciting to find half of Mercury covered with glazed patches, for it would be almost positive proof that the sun had indeed produced some 100 times its normal energy at some time in the long history of the solar system.

Future expeditions to the moon will gather additional information about these fragile glassy towers, and scientists will continue to explore ways in which they might have been produced. This is only one of the multitude of questions raised when men answered the one basic question—how does man get to the moon?

MASCONS

Another exciting question concerns the mascons, the areas of the moon where the pull of gravity is especially great. These places were first noted when probes were placed in orbit around the moon.

Mascon is a coined word made from the two words *mass* and *concentration.* The gravitational force exerted by a body such as the moon is related to its mass. If the gravitational force of a body is the same all over, then the mass of the body must be distributed evenly. Careful measurements, based on the data provided by lunar probes, have revealed that the moon's gravitation is not the same in all places. Around certain craters there are small regions where the gravitation is greater than in the surrounding area. This tells us that the mass of the moon is greater in those particular areas.

The same surface of the moon is always turned toward the earth because the moon revolves around the earth in exactly the same time that it rotates once on its axis. Geologists have suggested that the surface of the moon facing the earth has had a different history from the surface that is constantly turned away from us. They surmise that the surface of the "near" side of the moon is made of a crust of rocky material "floating" on denser rocks that underlie it. Perhaps at one time the crust was unbroken, as it appears to have been on the half of the moon that is turned away from the earth. We know very little about the far side of the moon, as all the rocks that scientists have examined have come from the side that faces the earth.

At some time the unbroken lunar surface may have been bombarded by large meteorites that punctured its rocky crust and then the denser, molten rock that lay underneath would have moved into, and sometimes through, the opening in the crust.

The surface of the near side of the moon is layered, at least in those parts of the Sea of Tranquillity and Oceanus Procellarum (Ocean of Storms) that have been explored. Perhaps a process somewhat like the following caused the layering. At some stage during the moon's formation parts of its interior may have been so hot it was molten, and the materials that now comprise it were all mixed together (except for meteorites that have since accumulated). Then, as the moon cooled, different minerals would have become solid as the temperatures dropped and pressures decreased.

According to this theory, for millions of years the moon cooled and the minerals became solid, some floating to the surface and others sinking. The process would gradually have caused the lunar substances to be separated somewhat as shown in the illustration. The lighter substances (feldspars) would have formed a crust, and the densest material (olivine) would have become

the core. Between these two formations there would have been a layer of lavalike liquid rock, the basalt discussed earlier.

Of course, this model is imaginary and oversimplified. Were it possible to slice through the moon, no one would expect to find such clear and neat separations—heavy, dense materials would be mixed here and there with lighter, less dense substances. In fact, a movement of basalt onto the crust has been proposed as an explanation for the puzzling mascons observed on the moon.

Scientists are trying to find out why the gravitation is greater in some regions than in others. One possible explanation is as follows. Solid basalt is heavier than the same rock when it is molten. There was molten basalt underneath the solid lunar crust. Suppose a large meteorite had broken the crust—in that case, hot, molten basalt under pressure would have flowed upward through the opening made by the meteorite. The molten basalt would have cooled, become heavier, and then sunk. But as it moved downward, additional breaks in the crust would have resulted, and more molten basalt would have risen. This would have produced a flat area with broken, uneven walls, and one made of the same material throughout.

This process may have taken place over and over again, so many times that eventually the flat region was resting on a firm foundation. These flat regions are the mares, the waterless "seas" of the moon. Later, molten basalt (lava) from beneath the mountains surrounding the plain might have flowed into a part of the mare, up through breaks in the crust. The newer basalt flows would have solidified in a local area, and that area would then become more dense. And so mascons might have been produced.

Many other questions raised by the moon rocks perplex scientists. Where did the moon come from? What was its origin? And what was the moon like during its early stages?

6

The Moon's Origin and History

The lunar basalts which the scientists in Houston and in laboratories around the world examined contained no hydrated (water-bearing) minerals, the minerals that would be present had there been any water on the moon at the time when the rocks were formed. This implies that the moon never contained any significant amount of water or that, if it did, the water was lost at a very early stage in lunar history. But not all of it, for instruments left on the moon by Apollo flights indicate that water erupts from below the surface occasionally.

Here on the earth, water has been present all through our history, and it continues to be the single most important natural agent in changing the earth's surface. Water dissolves rock; ice expands and breaks rocks apart; brooks and streams pick up stones, bang them together, and roll them along stream beds; ocean waves and surf pound the shore relentlessly, wearing down cliffs and reducing them to sand.

But the moon is essentially a waterless, airless world where there is no erosion or weathering of this kind. The only ever-present agent of change are the meteorites that collide with the moon, digging impact craters and causing changes in rocks by the high temperatures generated and by the force of the impact as they strike the moon at tremendous speed.

Since the moon rocks have not weathered very much, scientists have been able to study samples that may be from the original bedrock of the moon—among them one sample that is around 4.4 billion years old. And they have been able to consider more intelligently the various theories that have been proposed to explain the manner in which the moon originated.

For example, from their study of the lunar basalts which the astronauts brought back, some geologists believe that the moon was extremely hot at one time—not the entire moon, but to a depth of about 250 miles. According to these scientists, the core of the moon was cold. The heat would have caused melting at the surface, and minerals between the melted region and the solid core would have been in a semimolten layer. As the moon cooled, lighter crystals would have moved toward the top of the melt, and denser ones would have tended to drop down.

The composition of the breccias indicates that the lunar surface was extremely hot at one time, hot enough to melt rocks. But what could have caused this great increase in surface temperature while the center of the moon remained cool?

Possibly it could have happened this way. At one time the space around the moon may have been filled with meteorites, some of them weighing several tons. The moon may have attracted large and small particles that moved in at high speeds. The impact of these materials with the moon's surface would have produced heat, and if the buildup of meteoritic matter on the moon had been rapid, the heat would have been retained. The heat would have been greatest at the surface and would have increased as the moon became larger—the greater gravitation would have caused meteorites to be attracted at even higher velocities, and so there would have been even more heat.

Another cause for the heating of the lunar surface might have been the solar wind, which is not a cooling breeze but a stream of charged particles that radiates from the sun. When these particles intercept a planet (or the moon) electric currents are generated, and these in turn produce heat. The amount of current caused by the solar wind today is not even noticeable, but there is a possibility that during some stages in the evolution of the sun it produced a tremendous solar wind. If this happened, the electric current could have produced enough heat to melt the outer layer of the moon.

Radioactivity is another way in which the heat could have originated. It is possible that when the moon was created, there were scores of highly radioactive atoms that deteriorated rapidly and which do not exist today. These atoms might have generated tremendous amounts of heat. There may also have been radioactive substances that broke down more slowly, and so heating may have been very high for a short period and then dropped to a lower temperature for a longer interval.

When scientists consider the materials that make up the moon, and the changes that have occurred there, they also wonder how the moon itself may have originated. There are several theories to account for the origin of the moon, and although the moon rocks have not given the whole answer, many of the theories can be checked for probable correctness by studying clues in the moon rocks.

One suggestion is the so-called capture theory. This supposes that some time after the earth was formed, a mass of material such as an asteroid passed close enough to the earth to be captured and held in orbit by the earth's gravitational force. The capture of lunar orbiters by the moon's gravitational field, some people contend, supports this theory; they say that just as the moon captured these spacecraft, the earth could have captured the moon. But the lunar orbiters could not have been captured had there been no engines aboard to adjust their velocity; they would have been speeded up by the moon's attraction and would have ended up in orbit around the sun. Orbiters had to be slowed down at the appropriate time so that their speed was just right for them to go into lunar orbit.

Let us suppose that the moon had been an asteroid traveling through space in a sun-circling orbit. At some stage its speed would have had to be reduced if it were to be captured in the earth's orbit. It is impossible to conceive how this could have happened, for objects traveling through space continue to move at the same speed forever unless some other force acts upon them.

The capture theory makes it possible to explain the differences in mineral structure and composition between the moon and earth, but practically and realistically it seems to be more an explanation of convenience than one backed by solid scientific reasoning. However, at this time we cannot dismiss it entirely, because we do not know what might have happened during early stages of the evolution of our nearest neighbor world.

Other people have suggested that the moon may have been a part of the earth that split away. Notable among the proponents of this theory was George Darwin, second son of the more famous Charles Darwin. In the last half of the nineteenth century, Darwin became interested in tides and their effects, and in the rhythm of tidal motion. He reasoned that if at one time the earth had rotated very fast, making a complete turn in four hours, a rhythmical sloshing of the seas might have been started and that this, together with massive tides in the semisolid earth material, would have established sufficient force to break the earth apart, causing a large mass to spin off from the earth.

If this had happened one would expect to find essentially the same materials in the moon as are found on the earth, and this has proved to be the case. The substances that are dominant in both earth rocks and lunar rocks are oxygen, silicon, magnesium, aluminum, calcium, and iron. However, there are also, as we have noted, some interesting differences in materials and in the percentage distribution of materials found in earth rocks and lunar rocks. Perhaps these differences can be explained by the more rapid cooling that might have occurred on the moon after it was separated from the earth and cast out into space, or by its cooling and forming under airless conditions and under a lower gravitational force.

Still another theory—that of a common origin for the sun, all the planets, the moon, and all the other satellites—has been suggested by many scientists. According to this theory, the sun and planets were formed from a spherical gaseous mass that may have had a diameter of 10 billion miles. Many of the gases escaped from the system, and the remainder contracted to about half of the original diameter. As the mass contracted, it spun around faster and faster, and as the mass spun and collapsed, it also flattened and became disk-shaped. The diameter of the disk shrank to only 6 billion miles, and its thickness to about one billion miles. The larger central mass of material became the sun. Smaller concentrations of material in the disk became planets.

This is one theory about the formation of planets and stars (suns) from a mass of primeval gases. It is a small step to apply the same reasoning to the formation of the moon. Just as eddies might have formed into proto-planets moving around the central mass that was to become the sun, smaller eddies might have been captured by the proto-planets, and these may have become the satellites of the planets.

In their formative stages, the earth and moon lost all but a very small amount of the material that composed them originally. Early in its history, the moon lost all the gases that would have become its atmosphere. The earth lost most of the hydrogen and helium that surrounded it in its formative stages. Very likely the oxygen, nitrogen, and other gases which made up the original atmosphere were also lost. The gases now present might have evolved out of the interior of our planet.

Another fascinating theory of moon formation supposes that the moon was built up from particles that formed a ring around the earth. The ring was comparable to the rings around Saturn, except that it was much more massive. According to this theory, the diameter of the ring was some 130,000 miles, and the band of particles was some 25,000 miles wide. The particles in the ring may have been the remains of a primitive, dense atmosphere that surrounded the earth during the late stages in its formation.

As time passed, the sun may have flared into sudden, sharp

intensity, drawing away the lighter materials, and the remaining particles in the ring may have collected to form the moon.

This theory explains some of the observations made when the moon rocks were studied. The moon's density is much lower than that of the earth. A primitive earth atmosphere that became the ring would be made of less dense substances, since the denser materials would have been left behind on the semisolid earth. Also, the moon appears to be essentially the same at various locations, which would be in keeping with a formation resulting from ring masses.

Apparently the moon does not have a metal core. Here again we would expect that a primitive atmosphere would contain no metals—or at least to only a limited degree.

Elements that change to gases at rather low temperatures are rare in the moon rocks. The atmosphere of the primitive earth might have been exposed to high temperatures by sudden solar activity, temperatures that would have driven away these gases. On the other hand, elements that can withstand high temperatures and which would not be affected by the flare-up are quite common in moon rocks.

We've answered some questions about the moon—we now know the kinds of rock and "soil" that occur at a few selected locations on the lunar surface. But we've been unable to complete the story the rocks may be able to tell. We still do not know if the moon was thrown out of a proto-earth, if it was pulled out of the earth by a passing star, as has been suggested, or if it is a visitor from beyond the solar system, a mass of material that was captured by earth's gravitation. Moon rocks probably have within them the answers to many of our questions about the origin and evolution of the moon, and of the earth as well.

Answers to fundamental questions such as how and where the solar system came into existence still elude us. Actually the moon rocks have raised more questions than they have answered. This is what often happens when a great scientific discovery is made. For example, in 1905 Albert Einstein showed the world that energy and mass were related and that mass could be converted into energy. But how could such a conversion be made? Scientists took almost half a century to find out. Then they faced new and still unanswered questions of how to control the conversion most effectively and make the energy efficiently and safely available to do the work of the world. So questions lead to discoveries, and discoveries lead in turn to new questions.

As if they were working on a great jigsaw puzzle, scientists are fitting together bits of information about how our universe was formed and what it is made of. As they find more pieces of other worlds to study, their picture will become clearer. More samples from different locations on the moon, or from Mars, may give scientists the tools they need to unravel the whole story. But from just these few first pieces of another world they already have a better understanding of our universe. And they have discovered enough mysterious new questions to keep generations of future scientists busy seeking answers.

For Further Reading

Branley, Franklyn M., *The Moon: Earth's Natural Satellite.* New York: Thomas Y. Crowell Company, 1972.

Cherrington, Ernest H., *Exploring the Moon Through Binoculars.* New York: McGraw-Hill Book Company, 1969.

Cooper, Henry S. F., *Moon Rocks.* New York: Dial Press, 1970.

Gallant, Roy, *Exploring the Moon.* New York: Doubleday & Company, 1966.

Gallant, Roy A., and Schuberth, Christopher J., *Discovering Rocks and Minerals.* New York: The Natural History Press, 1967.

Mason, Brian, and Melson, William G., *The Lunar Rocks.* New York: Wiley-Interscience, 1970.

Wyckoff, J., *The Story of Geology.* New York: Golden Press, 1960.

Zim, Herbert S., and Sahffer, Paul R., *Rocks and Minerals.* New York: Golden Press, 1960.

Index

Aldrin, Edwin A., Jr., 1–11, 17
aluminum, 23, 51
animals, in tests, 30–31
Apollo 11, 1, 11, 33
  purpose of, 2
  samples gathered by, 3–6,
    26, 27, 28
Apollo 12, 21, 24, 26
Apollo 14, 21, 25
Armstrong, Neil A., 1–11, 18
asteroids, 40–41, 50
atmosphere, 52, 53

bacteria, 14, 32
basaltic lavas, 25, 29, 45–46
basalts (*see also* igneous
    rocks), 18, 20, 23, 24, 26,
    27, 45, 47
breccias, 19, 23, 24, 26, 48

calcium, 23, 24, 51
cameras, 4–5, 33
capture theory, 49–51
chromium, 24
Collins, Michael, 11
comets, 40
core tubes, 7–8, 17
crater rim, 21
craters:
  glazed, tiny, 26, 27, 32, 33–43
  meteorite, 23, 28, 47

cristobalite, 23
crystals, 20, 21, 23
  and temperature changes,
    24–25, 48
crystal structure, 19

Darwin, George, 50
density, 53
diseases, 14, 30–31
dolerite, 20

Eagle, 1
earth:
  age of, 26
  capture of moon by, 49–51
  erosion on, 37–38, 47
  gases of, 16
  gravitation of, 50, 54
  magnetic field of, 25
  meteoritic impact on, 29,
    37–38
  organisms in "tail" of, 31–32
  rocks of, 24, 30–31, 51
  soil of, 27
  water on, 47
Ellington Air Force Base, 12
epidemics, 14
erosion, 36, 37–38, 47

feldspars, 23, 44
Fiji Islands, epidemic in, 14

fines, 20, 29
formation of moon, 47–54
Fra Mauro region, 21

gases, 15, 40
   in formation of solar system, 52
   on Mars, 42
   in rocks, 19, 53
   in "tail" of earth, 31
geologists, 12, 18, 19, 23, 44
glass particles, spheres (see also fines), 18, 20–21, 24, 27–28
graphite, 10
gravitational attraction, 40, 42, 50, 54
   variations in, 43, 45–46
gravitational field, 13

helium, 52
hydrogen, 39, 52

igneous rocks (see also basalts), 24
   classification of, 20
ilmenite, 21, 24
   effects of temperature changes on, 24
impact rocks, 13, 21, 23, 29, 47–48
iron, 23, 51

lava, lava flows, 25, 29
LM (lunar module), 1, 4, 6, 10, 11
   engine exhausts of, 6, 34–35
Luna 16, 29, 32
lunar dust (see also lunar regolith), 1, 18, 30
   gathering of, 3

lunar orbiters, 50
lunar poles, 25
lunar probes, 16, 29, 32, 43, 44
Lunar Receiving Laboratory (LRL), 12–19, 30, 32, 47
lunar regolith:
   meteorites and, 27–28, 29
   zones in, 27
lunar rocks:
   age of, 26, 48
   collection of, 1–11
   gases given off by, 13, 53
   in laboratory, 12–19
   magnetism in, 13
   minerals in, 21–24, 45, 51
   possible hazards of, 14, 30–31
   texture and color of, 18
lunar sample boxes, 4, 6, 10
   opening of, 14–18
   sterilization of, 14–15
lunar "soil" (see also lunar regolith), 7–9, 14, 19, 27–29, 33, 35
lunar surface, 4–5
   temperature of, 48–49

magnesium, 23, 51
magnetic fields, 13, 25
magnetism, 19, 25
Manned Spacecraft Center, 12
mares, 46
Mare Tranquillitatus, see Sea of Tranquillity
Mars, 30, 41, 42, 54
mascons, 43–46
Mercury, 42–43
metamorphic rocks, 12–13

meteorites, 13, 25, 27, 45
  impact of, 18, 23, 28, 29, 35,
    36–37, 47–49
microbreccias, 20, 21, 28
microscopic study, 12, 28, 32
minerals, 21–24, 45, 50, 51
  hydrated, 47
Mission Control, 5, 8, 9
moon:
  age of, 26, 48
  bedrock of, 21, 28, 48
  core of, 45, 48, 53
  crust of, 44, 45
  life on, 18, 29, 30–32
  magnetic fields in, 25
  magnetic pole on, 13
  near vs. far side of, 44
  origin of, 49–54
moon rocks, *see* lunar rocks

nitrogen, 13, 15, 52
novas, 39

Ocean of Storms (Oceanus
  Procellarum), 44–45
olivine, 21, 24, 44
organic carbon, 13
organisms, lunar, 12, 31–32
oxygen, 23, 51, 52

pits, 20–21, 24, 25
plagioclase, 21, 23
planets, 30, 42–43, 49, 52
pyroxene, 21, 23

radioactivity, 26, 49
Ranger, 1
regolith, *see* lunar regolith
ring theory of moon origin,
  52–53

samples, 2
  contingency, 3–6
  documented, 7
Schiaparelli, Giovanni, 30
Sea of Fertility, 29
Sea of Tranquillity (Mare
  Tranquillitatus), 1, 28, 44
silicon, 21, 23, 51
solar-flare theory, 39, 41–43,
  53
solar telescopes, 39
solar wind, 6, 17, 49
stars, 39–40, 41, 52
sun, 49, 50, 51, 52, 53
  effect on lunar surface of,
    38–43
sunspots, 39
super-novas, 39
Surveyor, 1

tektites, 13
temperature:
  of moon, 6, 48–49
  in rock formation, 13, 23–24,
    25, 28, 34–35, 36–37,
    44–45, 47–48, 51
  of sun, 41
tides, 51
titanium, 21
Tranquillity Base, 11, 26

Venus, 42
viruses, 32
volcanic rocks, 12, 18, 24–25

water, on moon, 8–9, 47

zirconium, 24